THE WALL STREET JOURNAL.

Portfolio of
Business Cartoons

THE WALL STREET JOURNAL.

Portfolio of Business Cartoons

Edited by **CHARLES PRESTON**
Introduction by **ROBERT L. BARTLEY**

Published by

THE WALL STREET JOURNAL.

DOWJONES

ISBN 1-881944-19-0

Books can be purchased in bulk at special discounts.
For information please call (800) 635-8349, Dow Jones & Company.

The Wall Street Journal
200 Liberty Street
New York, NY 10281

Printed in the United States of America
1 2 3 4 5 6 7 8
First Edition

THE WALL STREET JOURNAL.

Portfolio of

Business Cartoons

"Choosing funny drawings," according to Malcolm Muggeridge, "is about the most difficult and hazardous enterprise known to man." Though loath to take issue with the fabled Punch editor, I must report that my recent foray into fifty years of The Wall Street Journal's "Pepper...and Salt" cartoons was a delight.

When the Journal's Vermont Royster – back in the pre-Eisenhower days – assigned me to edit the "Pepper...and Salt" column, he observed that there was more than enough earnest gravity on the editorial page. My mission was to provide a smattering of condiment for the weighty discourse in the adjacent columns.

Though we focused on the foibles of daily life, it was inevitable that the essence of the times would flavor our cartoons. The Journal's first drawings appeared during the halcyon days of Ozzie and Harriet, when women wore aprons at home and men were at work. Some of these cartoons are now discomfiting but are included as a record of those benighted days. Cartoonists, like other commentators, don't make the times; they merely record them.

Our selections provide a timely chronicle of fifty years of business history. For it is in the inkwell of contemporary events that the cartoonist smilingly dips his pen. Ponytailed executives on dress-down Fridays, nose rings and V-chips are all grist for the satirist's mill today – just as fintails, long hair and draft-card burnings were in the '50s, '60s and '70s.

It is tempting to enunciate an erudite comic theory or reach into the netherworld for a definition of humor. Mercifully, I will stop right here, so you can get on with the laughs, smiles and bittersweet dividends of five decades of Wall Street Journal cartoons.

CHARLES PRESTON

"PEPPER...AND SALT" EDITOR
THE WALL STREET JOURNAL

To the casual reader, The Wall Street Journal's daily cartoon feature, "Pepper... Salt" could scarcely be more simple and straightforward: an old-fashioned gag cartoon. To us old-timers at The Wall Street Journal, the feature is redolent of our history.

The headline itself we can trace back to 1915, part of a reorganization of the paper under the legendary C.W. Barron, who had recently purchased Dow Jones & Company with his wife Jessie Waldron. It ran over a collection of quips and verse culled from other papers. The feature took its present shape with the publication of the first daily cartoon on June 6, 1950. Thus the millennium is its golden anniversary.

This was part of another reorganization under an even more towering figure, Bernard Kilgore, the publishing genius who built The Wall Street Journal as it is known today. The cartoon arrived with the first blooms of "the Kilgore revolution." In June of 1950, the newspaper had a circulation of around 150,000. It had recently opened a third printing plant, adding Dallas to New York and San Francisco. It was to reach Chicago later that year, with the purchase of the Chicago Journal of Commerce. The "Pepper...and Salt" cartoon, in short, arrived at the take-off point of the Journal's ascent into a national, international and multi-media newspaper: with a circulation today of 1.9 million in North America, 62,000 in Asia, 79,000 in Europe, and more than 300,000 paid subscribers on the world-wide web.

The cartoon was pitched to Journal editors by a Columbia undergraduate named Charles Preston, who picked the Journal as a target because its gray and dull-looking columns were more in need of light relief than any other prospect. The timing was fortunate, since Kilgore and his editors were thinking of refreshing the typography of the editorial page. With the collaboration of the young Vermont Royster, later editor of the Journal, William F. Kerby, later chairman of Dow Jones & Company, became point man for the change. There was an obstacle, however, in the person of William Henry Grimes, the Journal's editor, the single most important person in bringing Kilgore to the helm of the company, and also a famous curmudgeon. The fresh new typography, and the cartoon, were installed while he was on a trip to Europe and presented as a fait accompli on his return. Thereafter, he talked about "Kerby's goddam picture page."

Over half a century now, readers have disputed this assessment, if indeed it was meant seriously even by Grimes. Surveys show "Pepper...and Salt" is read regularly by some 80% of Journal subscribers. Editors have learned from experience that they can skip a lot of things, but missing one cartoon will bring an avalanche of calls and letters.

Indeed, even at the millennium an obscure gag about "The Walrus and the Carpenter" brings morning calls asking for an explanation. Not that many of the gags are obscure. Charles Preston, still running the feature as the Cartoon Features Syndicate, sees to that.

"Pepper . . . and Salt" harks back to its origins in the heyday of gag cartoons, which then appeared regularly in such publishing powerhouses as the Saturday Evening Post, Look and Collier's. While in this more modern milieu cartoons are often harsh and dark, Charles still sends them back to the artists with instructions to draw in a smile, to make them lighter and upbeat.

This does not, I should hasten to add, avoid all controversy. Even the most innocent humor can sometimes offend, and it isn't always easy to keep up with which jokes are socially acceptable. The most controversial cartoon of all—debated back and forth in the letters column—presented a woman in an impeccable power suit telling a board of directors: "I feel if we buy a company and aren't satisfied, we should be able to return it." It came in 1988 (see page 95), a tad behind the curve of feminist consciousness raising. But Melanie Kirkpatrick, overseer of this volume and a feminist pioneer as a member of the first class of women at Princeton University, testifies, "Having recently gone through several thousand cartoons, I can tell you that if any class of readers ought to be offended it's successful, white, middle-aged men. In 'Pepper...and Salt,' you guys come off as real jerks."

"Pepper...and Salt" comes from, and speaks for, a simpler era—old-timers will say a more wholesome one. But its cartoons trip lightly into a new millennium, bringing a moment of mirth, and often insight. In the midst of the weighty concerns of the world and daily life, any of us can welcome the chance to pause for a chuckle.

ROBERT L. BARTLEY

EDITOR
THE WALL STREET JOURNAL

"Whatever you do—don't back up!"

"Take a postcard, Miss Hobbs."

"Happy birthday to you, happy birthday to you, happy birthday
Miss Gillespie, happy birthday to you."

"Mr. Clamwell has been expecting you.
He left."

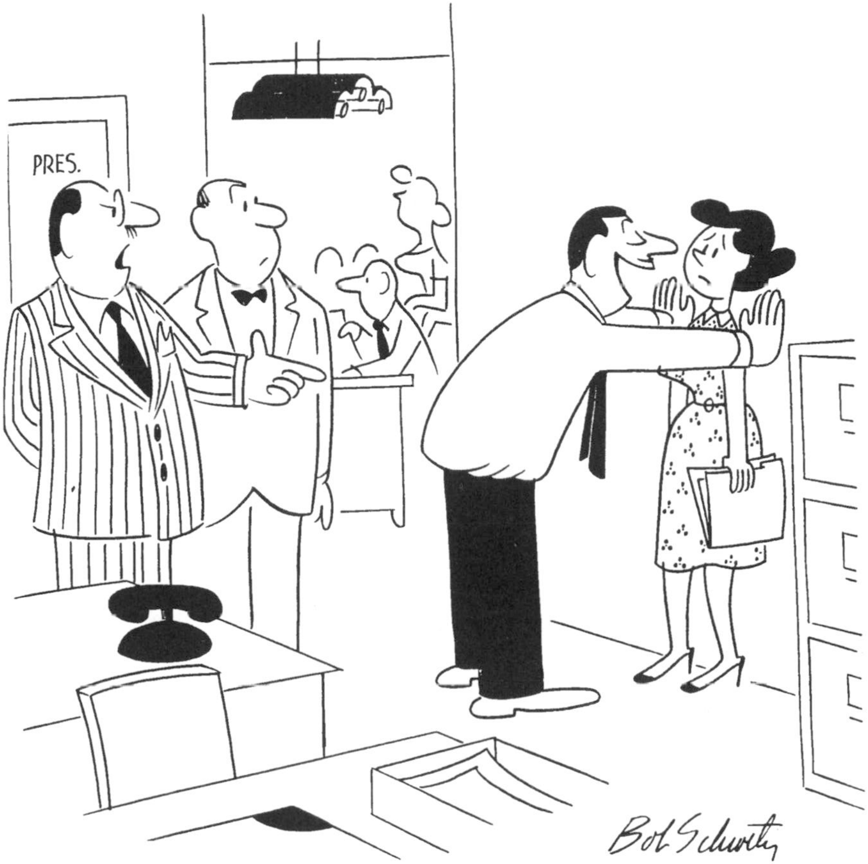
PRES.
Bob Schwartz

"Always selling!"

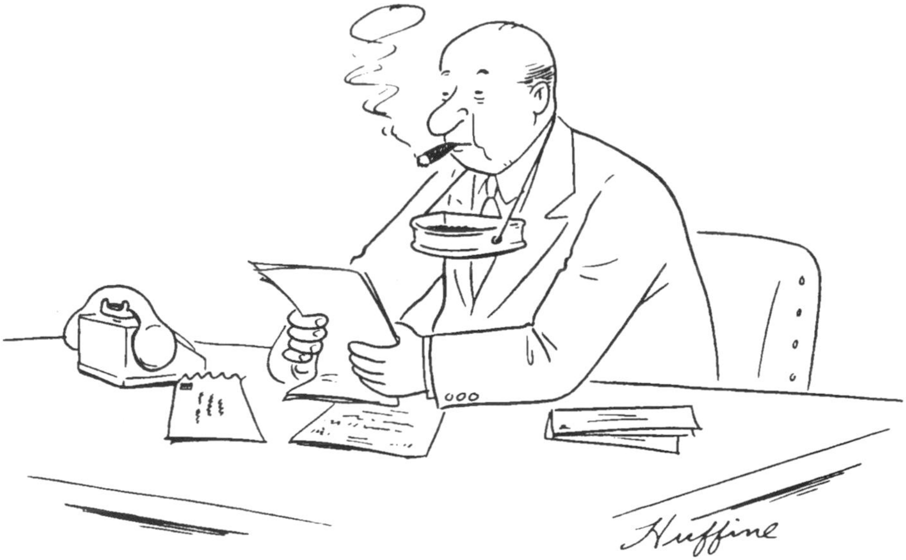
Huffine

"I tell you I had a rough day too!
This wrinkle-proof suit just doesn't show it."

"Is that a personal call, Dalton?"

"And pound the keys when you're typing that,
I'm mad."

"It's just one of those days when nobody feels like working."

"I'm always happy when the market goes down. Then I feel pretty good about the stocks I didn't buy with the money I don't have."

"I asked all the other girls in the office
and that's how they spelled it too!"

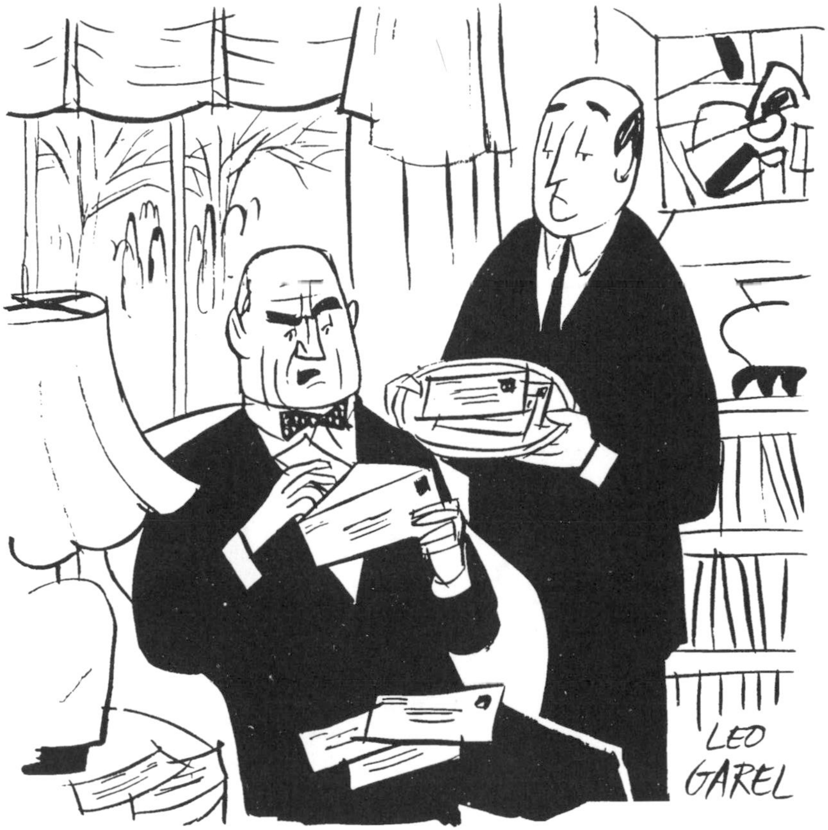
LEO
GAREL

"All I ever get is checks."

"When I said I wanted an itemized expense account, I didn't have in mind listing side dishes such as cole slaw and potato salad."

"If we can get a subsidy we can give this country
what it needs, a good five cent cigar."

"It could be just a coincidence, I suppose—but sometimes I wonder if it's the government's way of rubbing it in."

"I'd like to thank you people for coming in a half hour early for this special sales meeting."

"Will someone **ELSE** please second the motion?!"

"I can't understand it. People at my office
thought that story was hysterical."

"Mr. Hanson, we were wondering if you could re-arrange the desks so we'd be sitting boy-girl, boy-girl?"

"Sometimes I wonder what they do with the stuff."

"I knew you'd want to see all my receipts one day."

"Here's a few more things I want you to
clean up before I go on vacation."

"That's not just my opinion—it's yours, too."

"I'm tired of it all—drive off a bridge."

"I'm afraid I don't earn enough to dress this casual."

"I was hoping you could suggest a highly speculative
stock that always pays a dividend."

"All right, dear, I've got you aimed right at the bus stop."

"Which analyst do you want? Tax, stock or psycho?"

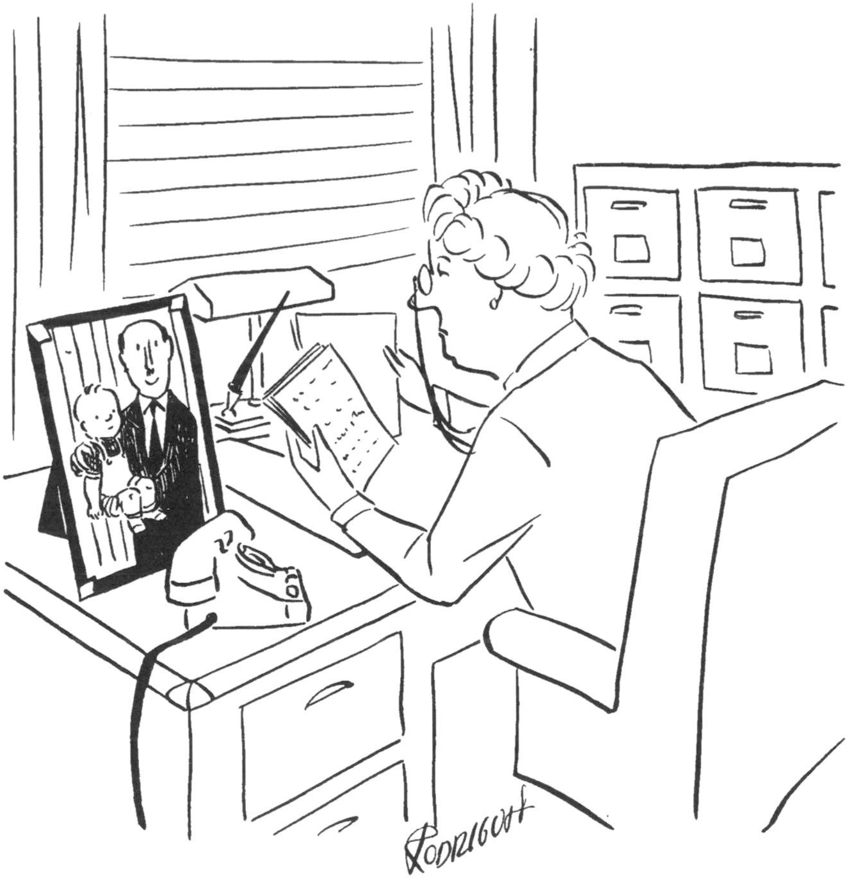
RODRIGUEZ

"The way I figure it you have to *look* money
to make money."

"These are just the trading stamps—
the groceries are out in the car."

"I'd like to help you up, Mac, but you know what
a strong union we have."

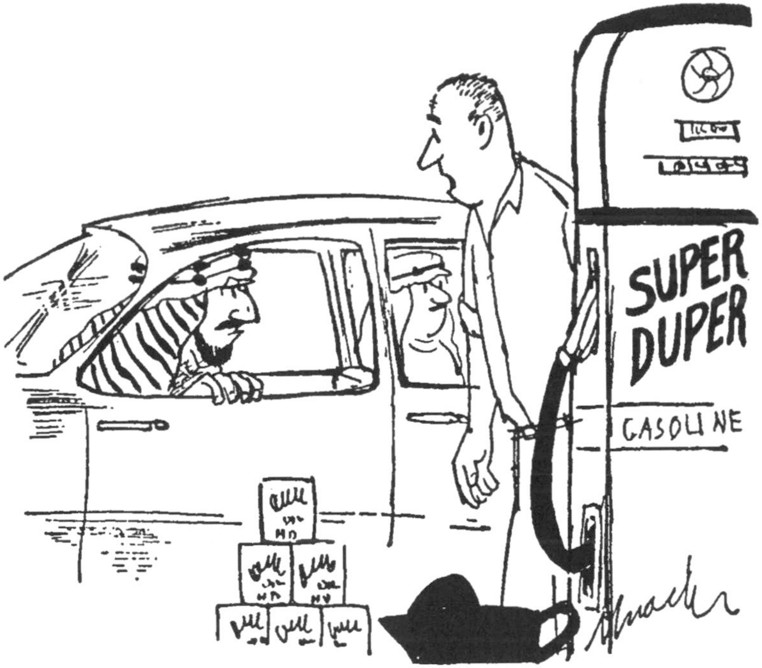
SUPER
DUPER
GASOLINE

"No, sir, I'm sorry sir. Our oil comes from Texas."

"Before you say anything, Daddy,
I think you should know he's making
$47,000 a year with his own rock group."

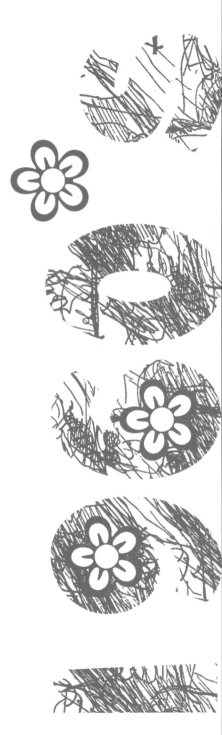

"I'm getting to be a nervous wreck, waiting for something defective to show up."

"Have you noticed any loosening of consumer purse strings?"

"No hurry on this, Wilberg—take all weekend if necessary."

"I wish the boss hadn't allowed women into the gang —
I can't get used to being called a henchperson!"

"This should shake things up — I've just found conclusive evidence that acid rain is caused by whales."

"In New York today, two conglomerates gobbled each other
up and disappeared without a trace."

"Hi, I'm a concerned citizen. Do you know of anything I should be particularly concerned about?"

"And to think all these years you've worried about some boy wonder taking over your job."

"I'm sorry, sir. You can't list a blown mind as a capital loss."

"Nothing thanks, I'm just reminiscing."

"Old Moneybags speaking."

"My next tune makes a statement about our high-technology, energy consuming society."

"When you see *me* in bells, Hasekell, *then* bells are in around here."

"**What's this your mother tells me, you want to become a security analyst?**"

"You know gentlemen, I find it terrifying
that we are the powers that be."

"You're the president of a corporation
that employs thousands of people."

"I have no friends—only contacts."

"I don't think you've quite caught what we're after, Bixby.
We want a soft sell, but we want a *hard* soft sell."

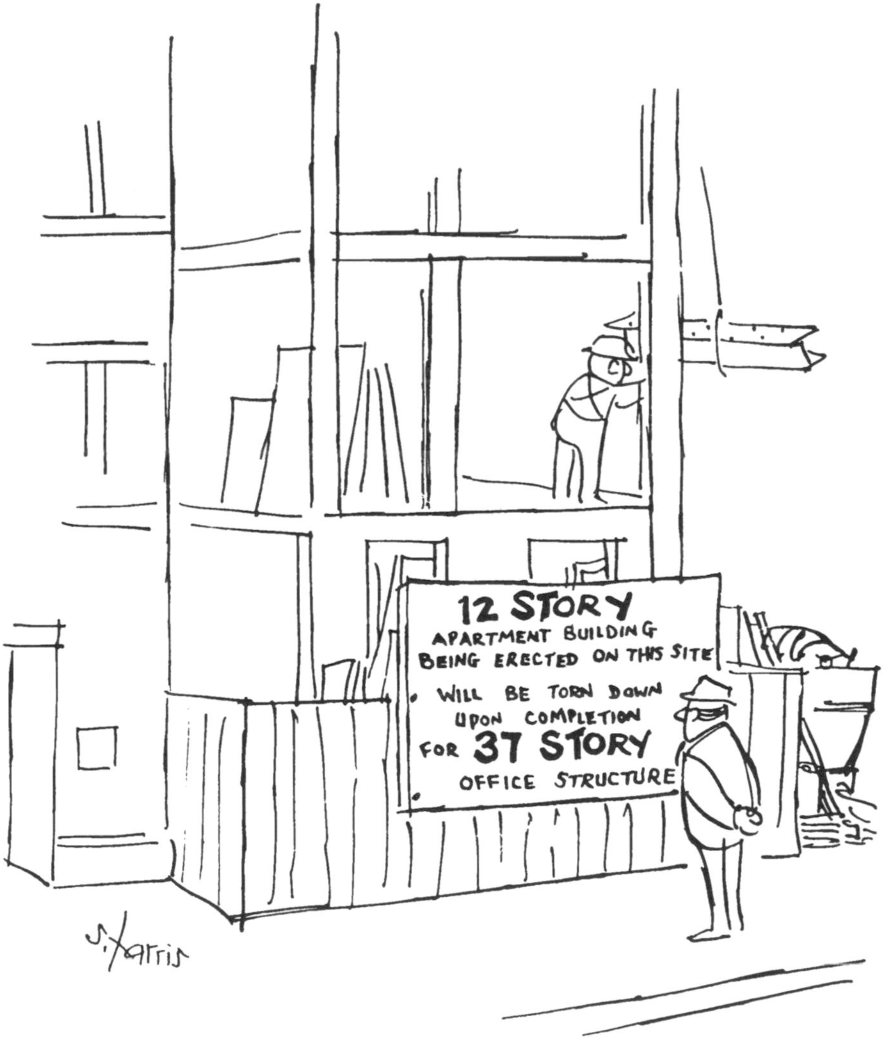
12 STORY
APARTMENT BUILDING
BEING ERECTED ON THIS SITE
WILL BE TORN DOWN
UPON COMPLETION
FOR 37 STORY
OFFICE STRUCTURE
S. Harris

"If you must know, I dress like this to be
accepted by my peer group."

"Insurance forms! Government grant forms! Requisition forms!
It was a lot easier being a mad scientist in the old days."

"Just sign on the dotted line and your industry will be deregulated."

"I know you want me to correct your spelling and punctuation, but what about your misconceptions?"

"If God hadn't wanted an oil depletion
allowance He wouldn't have created
an oil lobby."

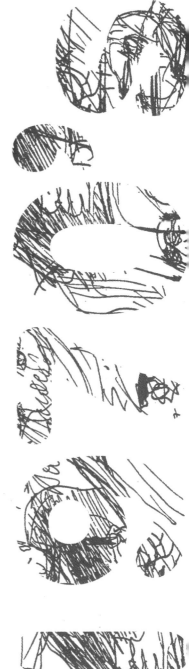

"Mommy has to go out to work, because Daddy can't cut it alone."

"I don't have any cash on me, but here's a $19.95 paper clip."

"Welcome to the new world. Please fill out
this environmental impact statement."

**"It's Mrs. Hawthorne. She wants to know
what sirloin opened at today."**

"You need a good rest—can you just wheel without dealing for a while?"

"We don't discriminate on the basis of age, sex, religion, color or national origin—we just don't hire Scorpios."

"And what will you gentlemen be writing off this evening?"

"Our people thank you, so much, for this purchase.
Would you like to be put on our mailing list?"

"In a complex court settlement, our parent company
gets custody of us on weekends!"

"Now they say we can't dump our industrial wastes in the river anymore. My God! What's a river for?!"

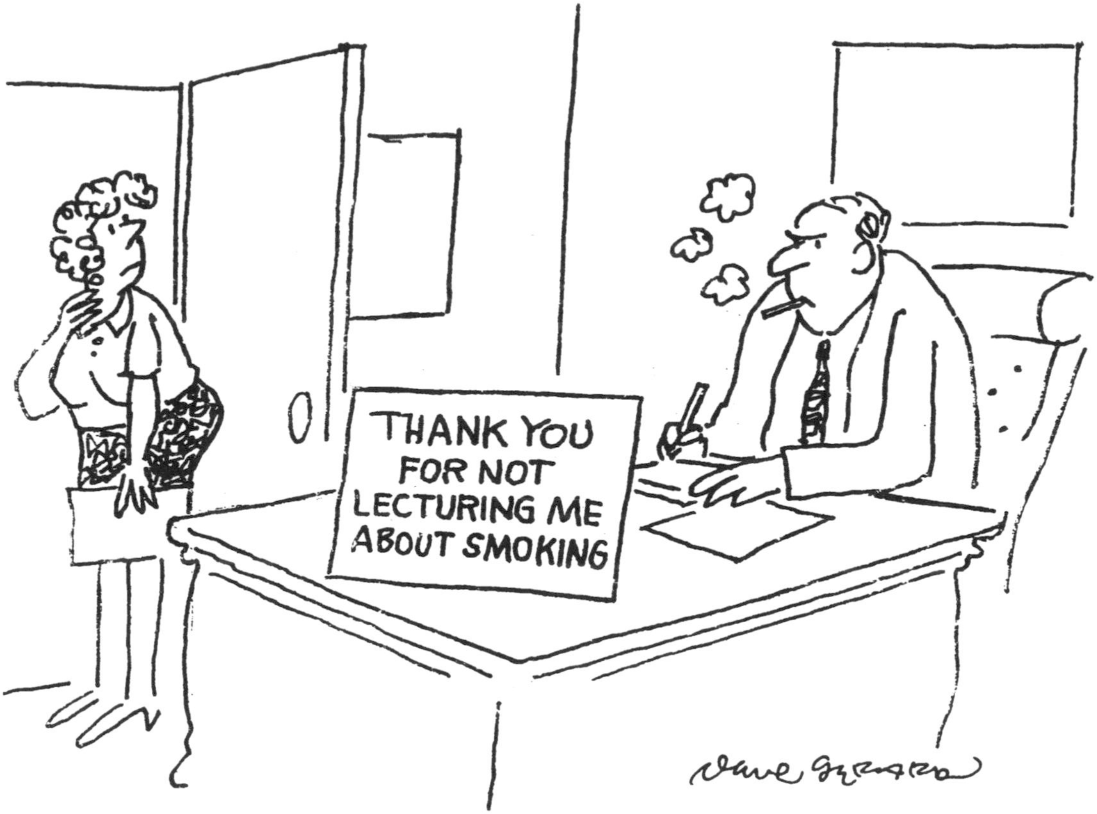
THANK YOU
FOR NOT
LECTURING ME
ABOUT SMOKING

"It's from the **Consumer Protection Agency**, demanding that we submit proof that the gates *are* made of pearl."

"I'm sure glad your Pa ain't alive to see this."

"Last week I'm running an electronics plant in Ohio—
today I'm a holy man in Kashmir. What won't my
tax lawyer think of next?"

"You've been gobbling up too many companies too fast."

"Look sharp, here comes the ol' man."

"When I grow up, can I be an Arab?"

"Say, sonny, if you really want to protest something—sing about the rise in the consumer price index."

"Listen! What was that? My beeper, my wristwatch alarm,
your microwave, our telephone or a telephone on TV?"

"I'm J. Calhoun Langdon who achieved, at the age of 37,
the presidency of Alpha Plastics; 12 directorships; multi-multi
millionaire and one day it hit me to discover what it was all about.
Now, I want to pursue this meaning and become one of the
best goddamn gurus in the business."

"I can't stand turnips–couldn't you pay me for *not* growing soybeans instead?"

"Of course she can handle them. She used to run
a day-care center."

"My, what a glorious day for a proxy fight."

"Sorry, but a mantra isn't sufficient collateral."

"I find this work truly fulfilling in many ways--there's the exercise, the sense of accomplishment, and, most important, the opportunity to make lots of noise."

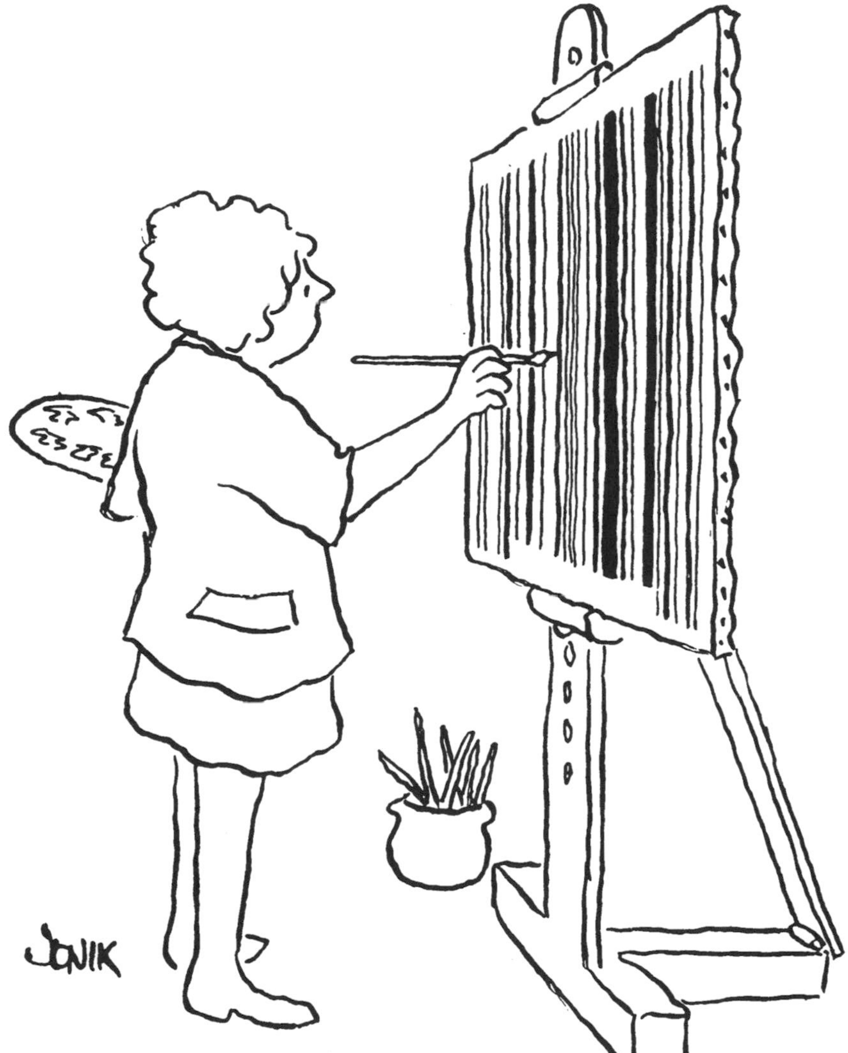
JONIK

"My name's **BIG JOHN** and I was brutalized in my formative years by a tyrannical father with whom I was forced to compete for the affection of my abusive, hostile mother ..."

"Ms. Ryan, send me in a scapegoat."

"May I have my allowance in Deutsche Marks, Dad?"

"On my vacation I'm going to do things I've always wanted to do—get a haircut, shave every day, wear a suit . . ."

"Certainly we're a minority group! How many multi-millionaires do you think there are?"

"Today the New York Stock Exchange closed early
to stop and smell the flowers."

"Frankly, I'd like to see this company get off the cutting edge."

"The Protestant work ethic isn't cutting it.
So we're switching to Shinto."

"We just don't speak the same language, David.
You're BASIC and I'm COBOL."

"I feel if we buy a company and aren't satisfied, we should be able to return it."

"I love being a partner Mr. Jenkins!
There's just one problem."

"You have acquisition fever."

"Something's wrong–I'm receiving a fax on my toaster."

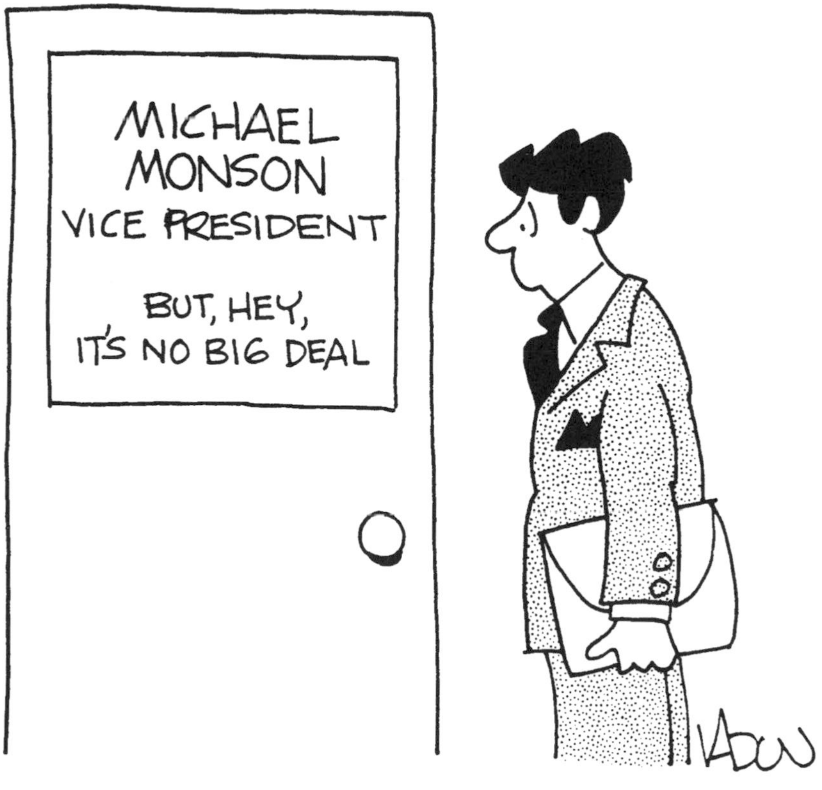
MICHAEL
MONSON
VICE PRESIDENT

BUT, HEY,
IT'S NO BIG DEAL

"Hey, Mom, guess who bought my lemonade stand!"

"You might want to stop trying to break
through the glass ceiling for a while ..."

"I always wanted you to make more than I did son,
but not on your first job."

"Stanley, just in case the takeover bid succeeds—
here is your poison pill."

"Can you prove it was a business orgy?"

"We're expecting stocks to rally but we
don't know which ones and when."

**"Number two, step forward and say,
'You can't lose if you invest in this stock.'"**

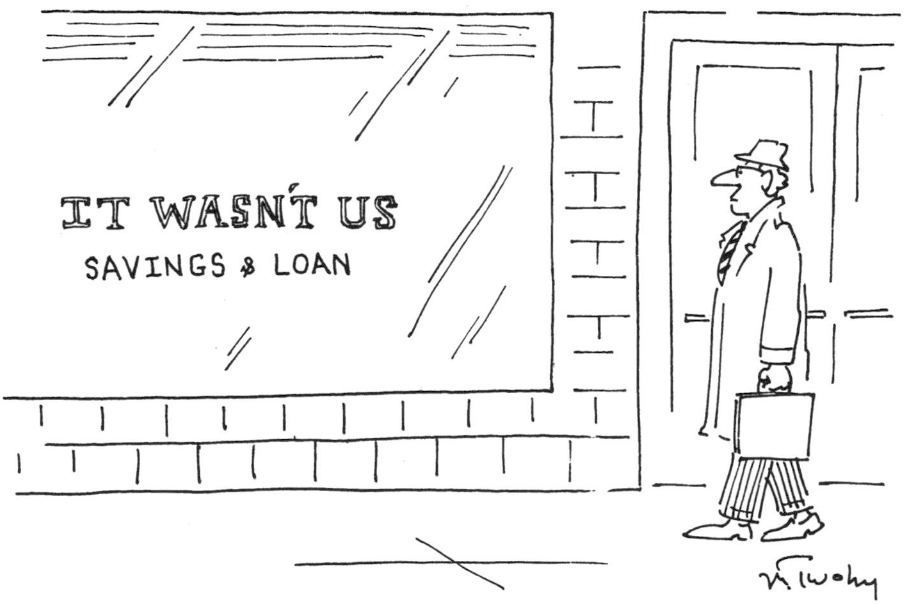
IT WASN'T US
SAVINGS & LOAN

"We finally found the American dream by
working for the Japanese in Mexico."

"My grandfather would turn over in his grave if he knew how many people are becoming filthy rich these days."

"I've got to go, I think I've got a bite."

"Our sermon today is entitled, 'The Meaning of God in a Bear Market.'"

"Grandfather, tell us again how you sold short in 1929."

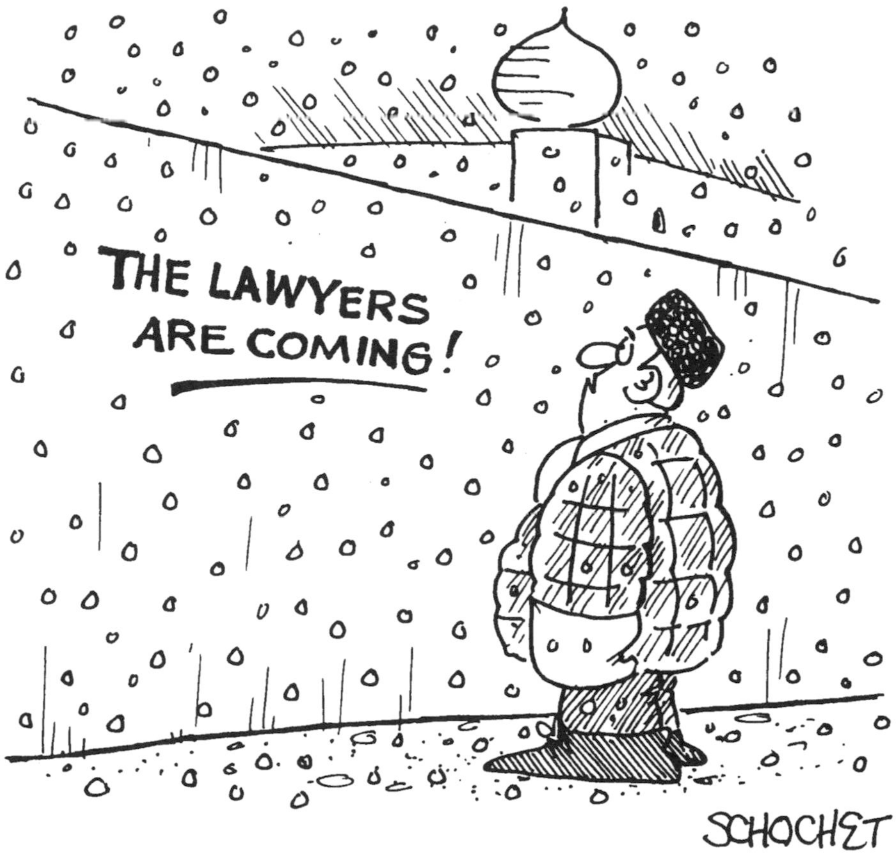
THE LAWYERS
ARE COMING!
SCHOCHET

"I'm sorry he's not available at the moment—both
Mr. Dobbs and his computer have just frozen."

"So I ask myself why do we offer a three-year warranty on a computer we're making obsolete after one year?"

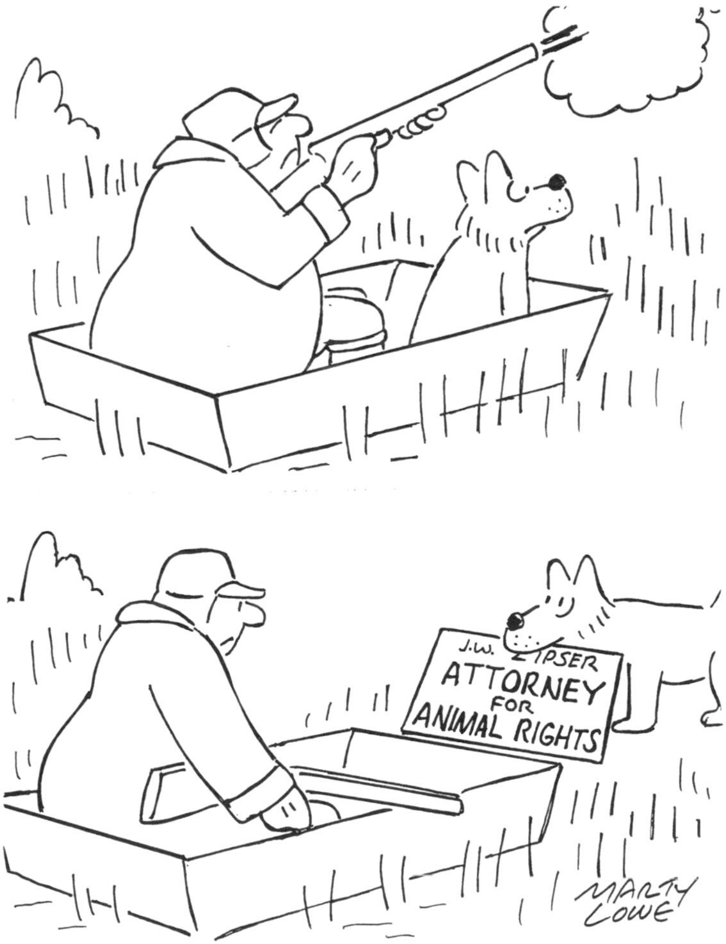
ATTORNEY
FOR
ANIMAL RIGHTS
MARTY
LOWE

"Let me speak to Freddy. He said he was going to be our waiter this evening."

"Well, I've got all the hardware and the software,
but I don't seem to have any underwear."

"I'm meeting with the boss in ten minutes.
May I borrow your barrette?"

"We're looking for someone who's excited about our product."

"That whining sound is common with Japanese cars
since they started losing market share."

"We're a support group for those who don't
need a support group but wonder why."

"Let's make sure that if there's a return
to morality, we get a piece of the action."

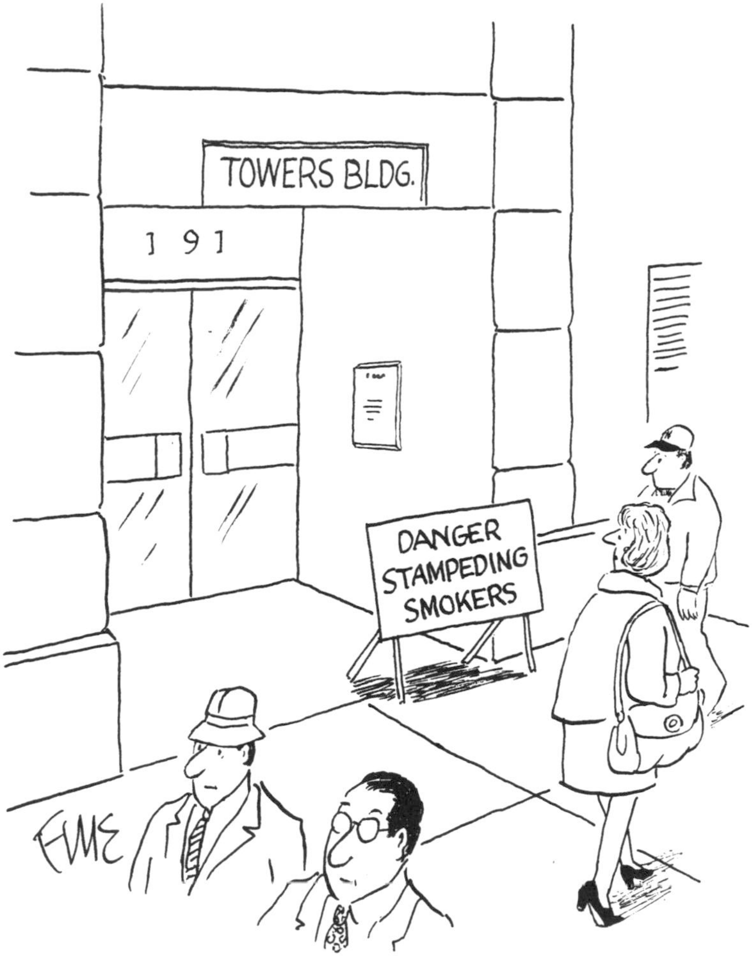
TOWERS BLDG.
191
DANGER STAMPEDING SMOKERS

"The reason for my trip? Business!
What other reason is there?"

"Ideally, I'd like to work at a company that shares
my sense of life's absurdities."

"Okay, one more investment strategy, then off to sleep."

"Burnout! You just started this morning!"

"He's back from his power lunch, now he's taking his power nap."

"Why do I need such a big purse? Oh, for 'girl stuff.'
You know—cell phone, pager, laptop, fax/modem ..."

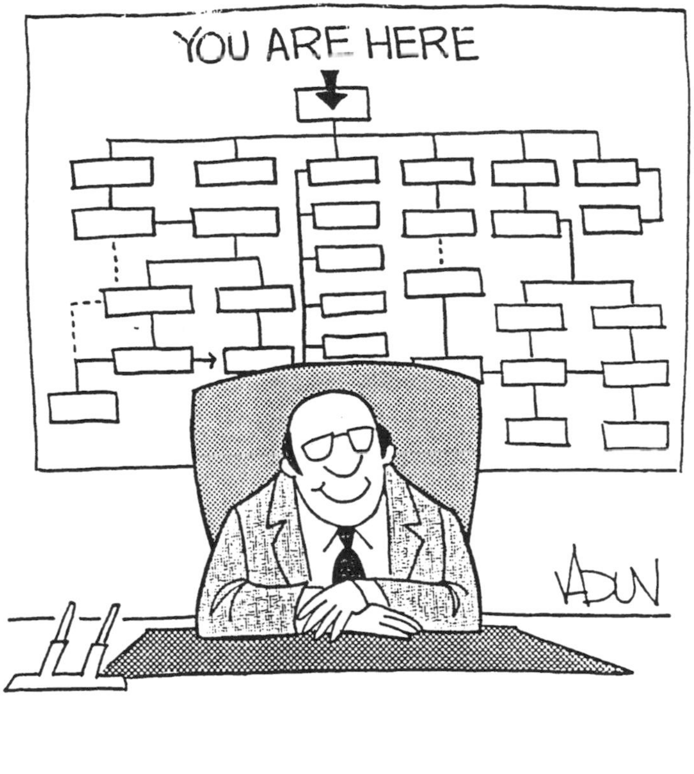
YOU ARE HERE

"The key to productivity? It's Fred, down in the shop. He makes stuff."

"South in the morning, north in the evening.
Why can't they make up their minds?"

"He just sits there all day,
waiting to chase the e-mail man."

"It's *casual* Friday, not *grubby* Friday."

"Family values rallied today, despite staunch
Hollywood opposition."

"The market has been erratic this week."

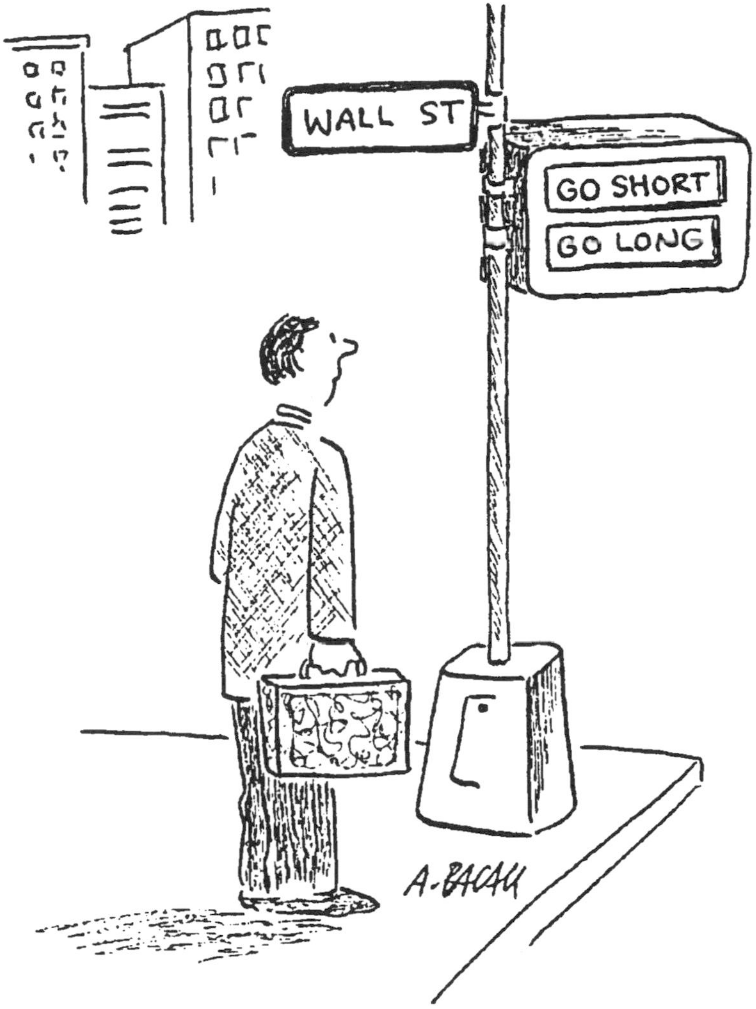
WALL ST
GO SHORT
GO LONG
A-BACALL

"This is man to man, Burkowitz. Leave the laptop out of this."

"Wire transfer of funds is convenient, but what
I miss most is laughing all the way to the bank."

"Did you really fire me, or were you just off medication?"

"Our factories are all out of the country.
All we produce here are very rich executives."

"It's the IMF. Can you come up with $25 by Monday
to help out with a third world country's payment?"

"Now here's a new ballad about choosing
a long-distance telephone company."

"We had the 'okay' to take 'er down when they thought there were only humans living in it. But then they discovered that spotted owl ..."

"I'm not one of those nerds who's made a fortune with some kind of software. I'm just a nerd."

"You *can't* take your business elsewhere, we've merged with all the other banks!"

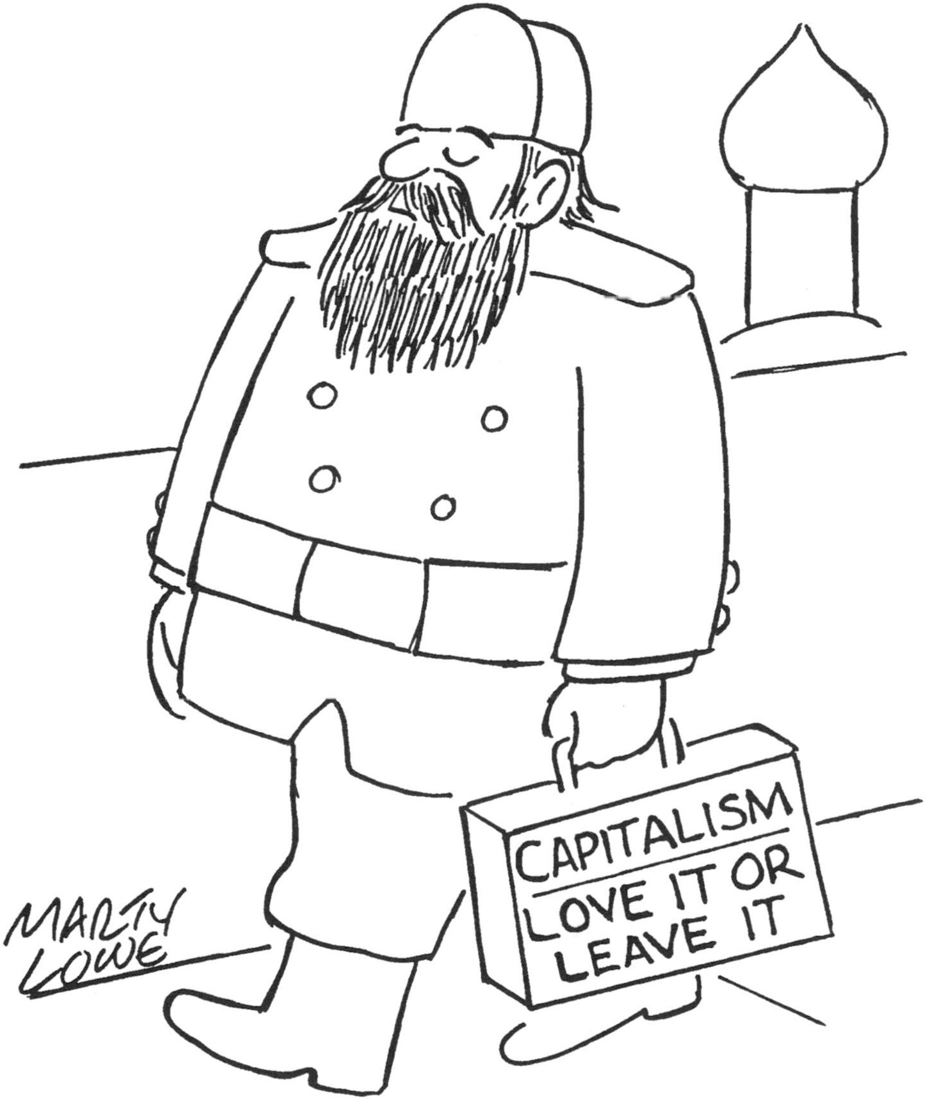
CAPITALISM
LOVE IT OR
LEAVE IT
MARTY LOWE

"It's e-mail from the patient in 914."

"I found the secret to happiness, but the FDA
won't let me release it."

"...and in a major medical breakthrough, we grossed $102 million in the third quarter."

"Could I interest you in a hedge fund?"

"It's no use Harry, I can't rhyme anything with condom."

"It seems they were on a conference call . . ."

"Chances are the fad is almost over and you'll just
be left with a big hole in your ear."

"Miss Jones, may I make a phone call to see how my mutual fund is doing?"

"I'll be good! Just don't return me to the main menu."

"We're both making money, so how could anyone call this a frivolous lawsuit?"

"Dad was in derivatives."

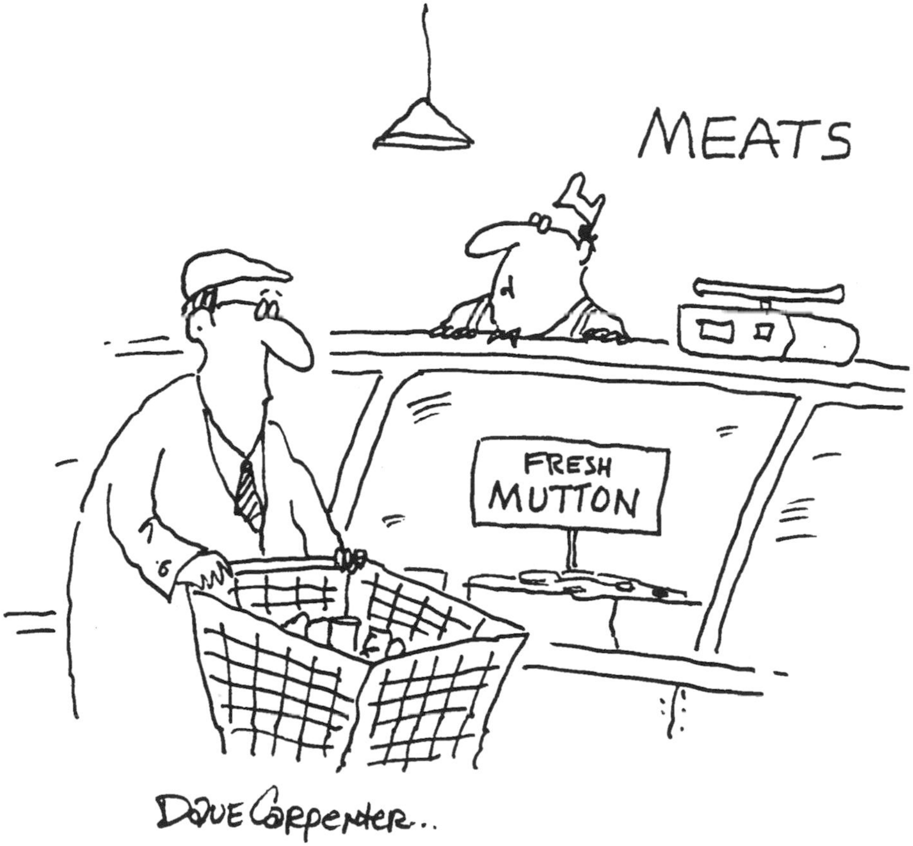
MEATS
FRESH
MUTTON

"Regular or cloned, sir?"

"We're under sixteen, but we're parents."

"Worshipping Mammon has been good to us, Horton."

"Oh c'mon, it'll be fun--let's all go down and
get tattooed and pierced!"

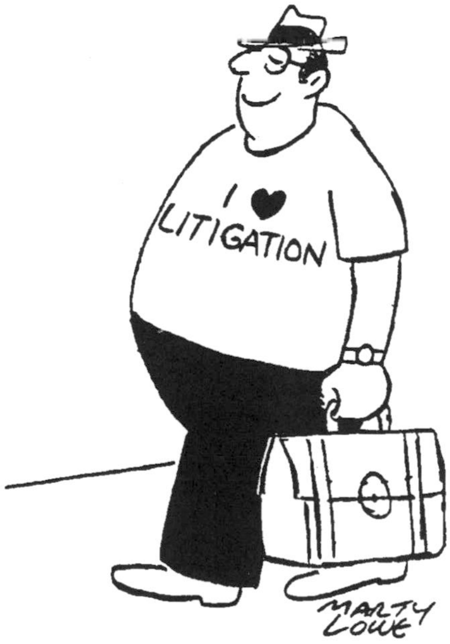
I ♥ LITIGATION
MARTY LOWE

"But I'll certainly keep you in mind
in case I ever take leave of my senses
and decide to entrust all my savings to
a complete stranger on the phone."

"Do we want take-out Cantonese, Mandarin
or Szechuan--or do we boycott until our
human rights questions are solved?"

**"Sorry--'Today's Dynamic Entrepreneur'
has ceased publication."**

"You know after fifteen years of high heels and ulcers, barefoot and pregnant sounds pretty good."

"Of *course* you'll accept a plea bargain . . .
I haven't tried a case in years!"

"Of course you can keep your pager here.
You just can't answer it."

"Why must we always take the same two weeks as Alan Greenspan?"

Index of Cartoonists

Acknowledgments

Thanks to Virginia Bubek, Ned Crabb and Melanie Kirkpatrick for their help in compiling this book.